IN CASE OF FIRE

Poems from the Blue Mountains

Edited by Michelle Rickerby

Illustrations by Michel Streich

SPINEBILL PRESS

Spinebill Press
Katoomba NSW, Australia
spinebillpress.com

A catalogue record for this book is available from the National Library of Australia

ISBN 978-0-6485315-5-5

Design and typography by Michel Streich
Typeset in Utopia and Myriad

The creators of this book gratefully acknowledge the generous support of The Blue Mountains City Council, City of the Arts Trust, who made this project possible

**BLUE
MOUNTAINS
CITY OF THE
ARTS TRUST**

blue mountains
City Council

This project is supported by the Blue Mountains City of the Arts Trust

Contents

Foreword

This anthology grew out of a need to play. To find joy again after the fires and the floods, and in the midst of a pandemic in an ever-changing world – and where else but nature and the arts will you find joy so readily available? But as is usual in times of crises, this moment also offered opportunity. To look into our own community and reach out. The Blue Mountains is a place of endless creativity.

In Case of Fire mixes the work of new writers with some of contemporary Australia's finest poets, featuring both previously unpublished material and poems you may already know from other collections. These works are full of wit and wonder. They strive to make sense of, or seek acceptance – and sometimes humour – in all the conditions in which we find ourselves. Conversely, they push back.

The poets and poems found here are by no means exhaustive, but sourcing material for this book has been a wonderful excuse to track down and talk to poets whose work I knew but had never met. I delighted in discussing civil disobedience and the social responsibility of poets over coffee with Phil H (sadly, I will never make a revolutionary), and the gorgeous suite of poems from John W which had to be photographed and transcribed when one version of technology failed and face-to-face meetings were impossible. Each poet led to another and another. I wish we had been able to do more. While this anthology is a collaboration of many, it would not exist without the energy of Michel Streich. Michel applied for the council grant that made this book possible, and worked with council during production. You will find his layout and designs add an extra layer of warmth and humour. It's been enormous fun to play alongside him.

The title, *In Case of Fire*, comes from a poem you'll find within, written by Mark O'Flynn, who kindly allowed us to use it. His is a work in memory of Deb Westbury, a wonderful poet, teacher and mentor who seemed to embody the very essence of poetry and whose generosity of spirit touched most, if not all, the writers in this book.

The poems that follow are listed in alphabetical order by title. We hope it lends an unexpectedness that aids discovery and surprise to each, even to those that are familiar. Every one of these poems sings its own song. Each carries its own particular appeal, venturing to stick its neck out and be heard – perhaps quietly, but never meekly. It has been a privilege and a joy to work on this book. I hope that it brings you, dear reader, moments of pleasure, and joy, too.

Michelle Rickerby

Aftermath

I tunnel twilight's shroud,
loaming down shadows,
to ferny floor.

Those cleft cliffs, stoic above
coal black stumps and blacker parrots
screaming as they fall.

Carol Major

Arrhythmia

I am the masked woman

sanitised and silent
in the waiting room.
I used to move in time.
A jerking puppet pulled by heartstrings

crooning to Talking Heads.

I used to be... I used to...
I used... I...

Singing is infectious. Choirs are banned, and dancing.
Police guard the entrances to public housing blocks
to keep the other out or locked inside.
If only 'the Covid' were as laconic and truncated

as Aussie slang.
But this pandemic moves to a frantic beat:
NSW pubs and clubs 300 pubs and clubs 300
pubs and clubs 300 pubs and clubs 300.

Something goes bump
in the night. It's the syncopated politics of the heart.

Sheridan Linnell

At D's Wake

You ask if I was there
when your father

blew up the family home
from bearded idiocy

and middle-aged desire,
but no,

I knew nothing of his affairs,
or how, behind closed doors,

he spoke foul words
to your mother.

Fear? I suppose.
Sadness? Regrets?

Yes, towards the end
he cried

like the baby that you were
when he left.

Craig Billingham

Autumn lunch

Sitting in a sideways glance of sun
wine numbed legs
attach themselves to autumn leaves.
My head floats above the screech
of sulphur crested cockatoos
and Sunday sounds,
to grey cloud
and the acrid scent
of summer past.

Faye Wilson

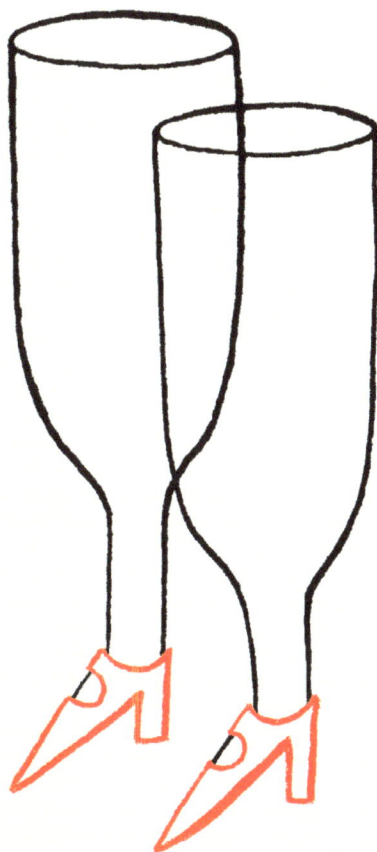

Blood and Bone

—after my mother came to me in a dream

spring creeps up out of a long low year sniffs the wire
where the fleece and old rags dangle retreats under a cold blast from the south

that tears the peach blossom from its branches
my hat from my balding head
as we walk arm in arm down some long boulevard where the first green

buds are showing

here and there in the gnarled canopy
and a kind of whispered prescience accompanies our amble the passing

cars seem to slow

momentarily
the dogs watch silent behind their iron gates

and there is a lightness in my step like childhood and the pain in my back

is gone
and the cruel wind carries a scent of lavender and jasmine and climbing rose

and turned soil in the dark fields either side

and her arm feels light as a feather threaded through mine and the cold

wind is snatching her words away
so I just nod like a flower and absorb her lightness
a bruised scent of jasmine amongst the blood and bone

Justin Lowe

The Blue Gum Forest

in memory of Rob Curtis (1972–2003)

Hush,
for it is not one,
but a forest of these blue gum trees,
and though not solemn,
they bid us be attentive
to the soft-fall of our tread.

Surrounded by these smooth
three-hundred-year-old trunks,
we are but saplings passing through.
And so, walk on silence,
listening as the bellbird's dip of notes
ricochets from valley walls.

I wonder what it's like to be inside:
to watch the mist unscroll across the river,
feel it snag in gentle folds of bark;
to be intimate with seasons
and the forked tongues of the weather gods.
Rain skates your skin and falls,
a benediction at your feet.

We set up camp,
grass strewn with gumnuts
that give eucalypts their name.
Eu-kaluptos, Greek for well-covered,
the capsules burst with flower
then harden to contain the seeds.
We too are soon well-covered,
by darkness, by our roof
of branches, leaves and stars.

When you chose this valley
as your final resting place,
I thought not so much well-covered
as well-concealed.
For under smooth bark, fissures grew
closest to the core.

These trees climbing into blue,
high crowns catching clouds,
remind me always
of your graceful stride,
as you walked among them
like a brother.

Vanessa Kirkpatrick

Bushwalking for Beginners

This is a popular walk with locals, best taken
once a week during moonlight. Terrain not too difficult
but includes a steep, stone staircase towards the beginning
unsuitable for children or the infirm.
First, open the door and step outside.
Already you will notice the air is different.
Sturdy footwear is recommended to navigate
the staircase, home to a variety of lichens and mosses.
Place any rubbish in the bin provided. Then grip bin
manually and wheel it down the length of the driveway
one foot after the other.
Caution is advised around the potholes
particularly if it has been raining.
Keep an eye out for possums active at this time of night.
At the edge of the road park the bin with wheels facing the kerb.
Take a moment to enjoy the view.
The stars are a highlight.
See the local wildlife busy cooking in their kitchens.
Their way of life is something we can never know.
Retrace your steps to the start of the walk.
Close the door.

Mark O'Flynn

Cicadas

growing underground for seven years
in the fleshy dark then forcing themselves
upward through the strong earth
they leave perfectly
round holes in the hard ground

their jewelled heads shining
the veined transparency of wings
they shrill for a day outside my studio
then leave

their papery husks clinging to trees
a delicate armature
for music dried up
and gone where?

her bones crumbled first
and then her organs
until she lay in nappies
slipping daily further down
beneath the sheets

beneath the winding sheets of stories
she slips a little further down each day
a tall thin iron-haired woman
leaning on a stick
her deep dry voice

understated and determined
calling me *my dear*
her white skin her nose a blade
improbable violet eyes

my aunt my art an odd half-rhyme
that twists around
the problem of embodiment
that we crumble and fail
our stories archived
in other failing beings
who sing them for a day
their papery skins
left clinging

Sheridan Linnell

The Clearing

high on abstraction & a
distance
of mountains we form a colony   the air is clean the water
rainwater
we have music & books & peace   on a radio we listen to the world
death itself & death itself & the cities be killed & ruined.

Michael Dransfield *The Change*

Surreal night   fog pixellates eyes   god
It is so transparent in the blue   *open them*   make   time a queen
Drove the fire still going, stoked   flares again while I make coffee
A tiger in the green pine, sunrise fur   where does the pine-cone go?
You ask   I look again   almost a breath at the window
How can I leave the moment you arrive   asking for milk?
Japanese maples sprout like grass   we dig the future
Branches over the springwater creek, wet brown leaf mulch
Red rain boots   velvet leaves drop propaganda over the flat island
Of violets   an abandoned colony of camellia flowers
Collapses as we pass   pure white perfumed flakes fall into pools
Of bracken water   a garden hose wound-up green in a bin of water
A concrete Diana decays   half-life classical

Next morning winter spills into us   sudden cold
Inside, a paper cut   I taste your blood for the first time   maroon rust
In brittle leaves   cold red stain in the dark grey sky
Keen iron we flow forever down the road   grass boats
Sent down the sun   you are the same as us   here we are
Look through glass at a sea of yellow   it happens in time
As great distant lights approach one another
Like snow flakes to melt at the same place   the clearing

I am already a hole in the world   you stop me
From walking   *Look at our shadows!*   my silhouette burns
A black hole right through the earth   one day I will perfectly fall
Into it   leading the way for you   I am sorry that with life I have also
Brought you death, a halo of darkness   we wave to the new darkness
As if it is nothing, & the world condenses   as reverie   perhaps
You will remember this: we once stood together over the road
Blocked the sun   laughed   a yellow daisy in your left hand
Making a world to make a self   the self is not the world   no
We move gold koi through the late lake of day   light falls
Shafts of amber coil into memory   the soft crimson fern   unfurling

Peter Minter

Crow

Here to see
York St rebuilding
itself in orange
bollards and gritty steel—
it bursts
from the maw of Wynyard Station
speaking crow and heroin
aiming to stab-jab-ab your fleshy lips—
to swallow your sweet-sweat
sack of skin, piece
by piece
while passers-by avert
their gaze;
their mouths
full
of feathers.

Michelle Rickerby

DOA

Is it true what they say—that Bo Peep shot
the sheriff? Yes, on a day called Roger
she did, she truly did & the river boss let it ride. Me,
I'd rather walk than ride; I'd rather be that proud wooer
in that dream about a guy called Hammer Black
who rescued his gal from the jackal master & it was
to the shame of his people (them people which was
so small, so very small).
      You'd think
a laugh would foil, but no, in this situation (a sham
situation) I simply showed some iron as fully-fledged
& got off with a slap, sock mom & shoe father
delighted that I'd shot no brain— a touch of class
in a perfect backwater moment!
      Anyway, good intentions
forsworn, that horn DID blow & angels DID come
to claim their own. Not me if that's
what you're thinking. No, 'twas Nanny White,
that nurse I met at the Raven Lounge. O how she wept
for joy as they carried her off.
      So nothing for it
but to change the sheets & weep myself. You want
I should help me home? That shoe
& a sun? A myself & a Thomas, a Thomas
& a true Nanny White? Not possible. Not mother enough
in me. What Bo Peep has in chasuble I'll never have
in chattel. So small among my people I've got
no goods to show.
      After Hammer rescued Bo
she shot the sheriff dead.

Philip Hammial

Driving Home at Dusk

Sky
over the mountains
full of cloud caverns, huge
banks of darkness
massing to the west, by the gas
station on Albion Street
the traffic-lights
glowing like emeralds, the dry
bones of the trees
as I open the gate
stirring at the forest edge, the cold
chain knocking against hardwood, nothing
itself tonight, mind
shut out of mind, the last
quarter of the waning moon
adrift over deepening flood.

David Brooks

Dugong

He comes from the sea—
bones carved by the wind,
the weight of his body
is crushing his legs
—*he is the mottled dugong*
beached on this mountain
trying to breathe,
the thin
damp air.

Faye Wilson

The Earth Dreams

I dreamt I gave birth to jellied eggs, tiny tadpoles, slithering
fish on a line
a hook in my mouth.

I dreamt I gave birth to pulped pupae, popped eyes, sticky
strings in a pot,
the syrup dark and thick.

I dreamt I was a half-formed thing
sickle moon fading
and me waking
gloveless on a frozen lake.

I dreamt I was a girl climbing a tree,
bark bubbling sap
to amber crust
the leaves feathering my face

I dreamt I gave birth to a shadow
that turned into crow's wings
opening and flapping over yellow fields.

I dreamt I was a crow in a tree, dreaming it had been a girl,
dreaming she'd been a fish caught in a pond,
the water webbing its way through creeks to the sea
and high above

nothing

and pale morning sky.

Carol Major

the end of winter

eyes to the ground
i walked beneath it everyday,
i never looked up.

i walked alone, crowded,
escaping his bad weather,
and one wet morning
i marched with damp socks
through muddy grass,
face first into a hands-in-pockets
shoulder-scrunching wind.
my eyes watered.

that day i noticed
grey on grey, above my head,
the nest abandoned,
noticed the light behind
the latticed lace
of what was left,
nestled in the bare limbed tree.

it was the end of winter.
nothing was feathered.

somewhere I couldn't yet imagine,
                                    birds flew.

Emma Brazil

Grasshopper, 1889

Stuck fast
the grasshopper in Van Gogh's painting
Olive Grove has achieved some immortality,
at least so far as it goes for grasshoppers.
Like sacred ibis preserved in pyramids,
Pharaohs eviscerated, or thylacines embalmed
with formaldehyde there's something
to be said for a modest tilt at eternity.
Disguised in impasto the grasshopper
has become a stroke of genius
on the path through the olive grove
towards the asylum, a sunny day
casting purple shadows on the ground,
the canvas itself *smelling of the soil*
as a good landscape should.
One daub of paint, no less lumpy
than the next, as was his style,
buried within the camouflage of olives.
Perhaps it speaks of the painter's frenzy
that he didn't stop to pick it from the scene
this mire of brush strokes
but forged ahead into the vision's depths,
its exquisite mummification.

Mark O'Flynn

green dresses

Up north we swam naked, everyone
drank ginger wine from dirty glasses
beneath mango trees in the afternoon and
dropping out felt more like
diving in, head first.
I ate fruit from trees and
smelt jasmine everywhere.

Up north I slept to the ocean's purr
and woke to cicada's song and
each day sparkled and
beneath my feet
the green earth throbbed.

Up north, the doctor
gave me his copy of the Kama Sutra
with my prescription for the pill
and everyone smoked too much
and on New Year's Eve at the beach
everyone kissed everyone else
under a purple sky full of stars.

Up north we swam in tea tree lakes
so still the water reflected sky,
glided past water lilies
growing from mud,
laughed to each other as dragonflies
landed on our nipples
as we lay on our backs and
floated on clouds.

Emma Brazil

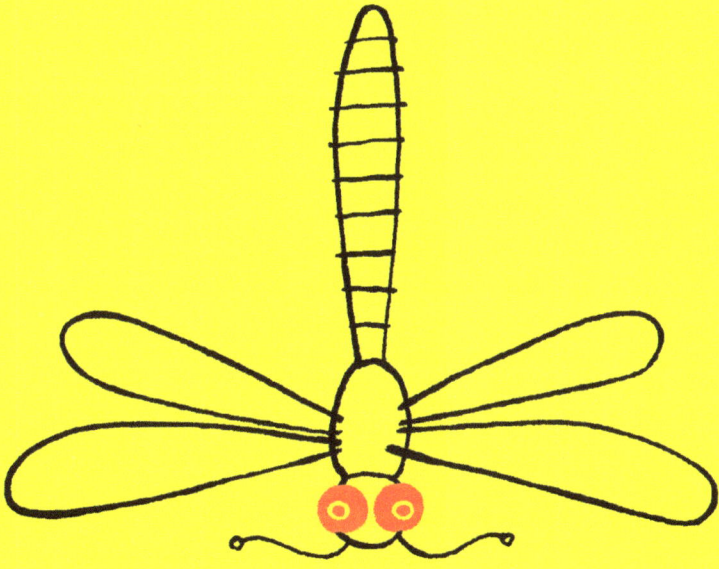

Heart Sayings

Heart of butter, heart of bone
Heart of silver, heart of stone
Heart of willow, heart of wire
Heart of somnolence and fire
Heart of hummingbird and hawk
Heart of terror, heart of talk
Heart of woman, heart of man
Heart of catch me if you can
Heart of double-decker bus
Heart of every one of us
Heart of hunger, heart of earth
Heart of child at her birth
Heart of sentimental nerve
Heart of echo, heart of curve
Heart of carbon, heart of clay
Heart of answer and allay
Heart of owl above the fell
Heart of bracken, heart of bell
Heart of use, heart of season
Heart of elemental reason
Heart of eaten, heart of grave
Heart of got, heart of gave

Heart of kernel, heart of turn
Heart of house beyond the burn
Heart of sympathetic wall
Heart of kindle, heart of call
Heart of sister, heart of mother
Heart of father, heart of brother
Heart of bowerbird and hen
Heart of wattlebird and wren
Heart of line, heart of word
Heart of accidental third
Heart of evidence and hold
Heart of colour, heart of cold
Heart of knot, heart of no
Heart of leave before you go
Heart of skew, heart of match
Heart of thistle, heart of latch
Heart of lamp, heart of lake
Heart of give before you take
Heart of type, heart of kind
Heart of book, heart of mind
Heart of emphasis and care
Heart of solitude's repair
Heart of old, heart of new
Heart of dial, heart of dew
Heart of leaning into sound
Heart of lost, heart of found

Kate Fagan

Hootenanny

No friend of crow we're phlegmatic.
You therefore can assume that we know what Honky will say
one hair apart. At which distance sewer stink
is an unlikely anthem. Not for us to sing, we're just
happy-go-lucky boys with a corpse
on a leash. Watch as we make our way
through the cafe crowd due cappuccini
& pay no mind to the tanker crunching its way
down George Street. If you insist you can come close
& compare our legs, mine & Joe's (which apparently
is the dead guy's name). Of his numinous face
should we bid adieu? Should we forget that lay-by Bible thang
with its would-be Gregorian chant? By this time tomorrow
we'll be hop & skip; we'll be booming, as loud
as maids at prayer!—Ray (that's me) & Joe
as tune-perfect as whales in trees! But, sung, what will
our mothers say? And who will discipline us?
And the tanker's captain up there on the bridge
will he pipe us aboard?—wayward sailors
after a night on the town. Gloat
if we may & we must, our offer to cleanse
those souls refused. So? So crow will have us
pneumatic, full frontal-exposed with a leg, just one
on which to stand while we sing.

Philip Hammial

Hope Stone

Cento for Felix Minter

The birds are at home
beneath a curved wall,
are a picture of an echoing hill.
Words like the angled dark,
salt letters, a boat hurled
to the ground. Seek your cradle
near three brilliant stones
(slow wing beats and the jangle
of a spoon). What do they know,
birds in their nest? You shared breakfast
with a notebook and a moth.
Come on wings of joy
Come & make thy calm retreat
Come the studious hours of deep midnight
Flying upside down
between dews and barks,
eyes half-open.

Kate Fagan

The Illustrator's Handbag

for Liz Anelli

The illustrator carries an ocean and in it
nightjars soar.

She shoulders memories; dangling on a stick
like a string of glittering fish.

These memories swirl and storm,
but even if you shake them

—as a snow dome—they remain
discrete as confetti,

each labelled: a digital specimen
found + found + stored.

The cartographer carries her world in her pencil
case and sketch book.

She is all the unusual things
she collects.   Inside, her

family floats on flotsam—
gum wrappers, strings of hair

and emergency biscuit crumbs. Daily she dives
into the ocean, wrestling the inky void.

Michelle Rickerby

In Case of Fire

(*i.m. Deb Westbury*, 2018)

Rain skates
across the roof tops
blackening tiles, numb to all the predictions of rain. It offers universal
foil to dignity, ruffled feathers, wedding hats, washing weeping
into the thin space between chimney and clothes horse drying by the fire.

In the corner
a cardboard box
and in the box, wrapped in a shamrock tea towel a scorched baby possum
fallen down the chimney into the squealing flames. Next night and the next,
the mother possum returned, screeching down the chimney's hot throat.
The vet said it would not survive, but it did. Everyone else goes on.
Only you don't.

Walking home
from your house
I saw more uncollected species of birds than I have ever seen before.
All those parrots in their feathered trousers, the dusk that follows every bird
to its mystery, the ambush of each footstep like a street sign pointing two ways.
It might have been the wine, it might have been the grief welling behind
a future hour, that is, drop by drop, filling this room to the cornices.

The dust
of your voice
on my answering machine, a message received too late. Your phobia
comprehended; I don't think it has a name beyond suffering, manifest
in refusal to answer the phone. Nothing good ever comes of it. Bad news
crouches in your ear and will not leave.

Rain will not
douse the past.
Before you wake first you must drown. Only once I saw you struggle
through the bush. It was the tiny florets held your interest, not the grand
scale of the path, dimension of the journey back – that was for symbolists
and wankers. I asked once if you liked music and you said: 'Fuck no.'

The piano
in the corner
silent against the inside wall of the lounge room, clunking, you claimed,
as if being abused by a primary school teacher. I never heard you play.
So much of your life left to wayward imagination. It might have been different.
It might not have been different. It might have been worse.

It was. It is.
You are.
I know some of the houses where you lived, one in mournful earshot
of a donkey. The mutual understanding you had with the koori boys who'd
steal your car, and from whose house around the corner you'd steal back,
leave them a bottle of beer for looking after it. A little splosh.
The dearth of kindness in the world.

Here are the ashes
of your son
in an urn on the mantelpiece, beside your bed, where ever you are.
When the fires came I packed my books and important documents
necessary to explain my identity, a few clean clothes, photos, a toothbrush –
car of random possessions if and when the order came to flee.
Mother of these ashes, you packed your urn.

The skeleton
of a leaf
will do as a book mark. The bisected nautilus, plumes of coral and collected
South Coast shells adorning the bathroom window sill, an archipelago
of biography. Each one the story of its place in your life.

Then the rain.

Mark O'Flynn

Incident at Mt. Boyce

around those notorious hairpin bends
gauntleted by broken barricades
it takes half a dozen fire engines
first to light, then to supervise the incineration
of a trail of scattered beehives
littering both sides of the highway

and, at the end, where the winding road
straightens and starts to climb Mt. Boyce
the now bankrupt apiarist, beside his empty
Bedford tray, head bowed in dismay,
straddling the verge in sweet waxy smoke
rues the craftsmanship of his clumsy knots.

Mark O'Flynn

Last Leaves Fall

Last leaves fall
and in bare branches
this twigged bowl
I feel must be saved
for the industry in it
for the moulded mud
for the scraps of blue shell
for all the walls I've painted
the curtains made
Lego blocks tidied away in a box
and this empty tree waving its scratchy arms.

Carol Major

Last summer

for Sasha

Last summer
the earth so parched
I could not imagine a single seed
turning to green.
I could not imagine.

Heat pulsed its drumbeat –
an army approaching
and sly propaganda of smoke
crept into each kitchen, each bedroom,
each hallway of thought.

What else could we speak of
when we woke to smoke
thick on our tongues,
thick on the rooves of our mouths?

Last summer
as families walked into the sea
and the flight of galahs
lay charred on the smouldering ground,
I realised I had no clothes
fit for battle – only
this thin cotton shift
I have worn since my childhood.

Fragments of self dispersed –
dry leaves in a windstorm.
I could not gather the leaves,
hold them securely enough
to write down a list,
pack my life into boxes,
get into the car.

And where could we go
when our country, our state,
our village was burning?
When leaves were falling
as far as New Zealand,
when ash-clouds were clawing
the Chilean coast?
On the last day of last year
a mushroom cloud bloomed
at the end of our road.
As the flames licked closer,
my heart beat louder than sirens,
louder than choppers slicing the air.

All I knew
was to keep you safe –
to guard the one hint of green
that had fallen and grown
in the loam of my heart.

Vanessa Kirkpatrick

Linden

after Edward Thomas, 'Adlestrop'

Linden? The station? Yes, I remember
The sign, because early one Saturday,
Unexpectedly, the Bathurst train lay
Briefly over there. It was late November.

The doors opened. Someone coughed.
No one boarded or stepped off
Onto the long, quiet platform. What I saw
Was 'Linden', nothing more,

Except golden coreopsis, long rows
Of dry sansevieria, a few clouds high
In the pale sky. And for those
Few moments, near-by,

I heard a currawong call,
And around her, it seemed, in bands
Ever wider and wider, all
The birds of the Central Tablelands.

David Brooks

Lockley's Pylon

Running
hunched over and wet
between thunder claps and lightning
—on my path,
emerging out of mist
symmetric blooms
on hectic zig zag branches,
burnt black and
hung with crystal-beaded spider webs.
Yawning above,
great waves
of half-swallowed sandstone
pull at me—
beside the track
fresh Isopogon anemonifolia
like small yellow fireworks
whorling outwards,
minute opalescent pearls podded inside
the unfurling fronds of ferns.
Soaked with rain
scared,
stumbling and breathless
for one moment
I am immeasurably happy.

Faye Wilson

Margaret Mead on Manus Island

Married to Fortune, Mead returned again and again
to the island and the village of Pere.
She gave pen and paper to the children,
small ethnographers who caught
local fish and customs in their pencilled nets.
She and they refuted Piaget and primitivism, colonial powers
dressed up as the universal.
She watched how the sons and daughters of Manus
rode on their elders' shoulders
holding their fathers' throats in a loving choke.

On Manus Island, Mead broke her right ankle for the second time.
The village bonesetter patched her up,
villagers built her crutches from canoe poles and wooden pillows.
She designed and wore a fieldwork dress with pockets
large enough for her notebooks
and a wrap-around waist to accommodate change.

Mead thought Manus a successful model of cultural transformation
(Twenty five years of rapid technological change, new lives for old)
supported the 'untutored revolutionary genius' of Paliau
who resisted the tuna canning industry
and 'flying-fox' politicians who come only for the ripest fruit.

Mead had her critics. Because rather than in spite of this,
I reach my white hands
—that, like hers, are not innocent—
into the deep pockets of my fieldwork dress.

We have come like flying foxes
to feed once more on the fruits of others
to commit the violence of terra nullius
to turn an island into a prison
for those who seek refuge and survive the seas.

Small ethnographers with coloured pencils
capture birds in cages
tears on rudimentary faces
worms wriggling in a plate of food
families caught behind a wire grid
the sun shining and scowling
one stick figure beating another with a stick
one man hanging
one girl smiling
as someone braids her hair.

Sheridan Linnell

Mektoub

My face down which
mascara runs, a pool of it. So much
for the flapper years. So obsequious those ancients
they'd drop me a horse, a rocking-horse that rocking
hoofs up the stink of a book, one of mine that Charles
& the Chatter Boys, the bastards, are in sing-along
making a mockery of. Never mind, they'll get theirs
in a year or two: Chuck & the Titter Boys as laughable
as an oatmeal endeavour in a minstrel show. Go ahead
show & tell: what DID the x-ray show? — that swallowed
tooth, No, it's not some saint's, a relic that could fetch
a grand or two. Then whose? Could have happened
when I met my nemesis in that pole dance routine:
down with a crash.
                          First
you got your hair & then your tongue entangled with
some other fool's. And now: Hootchy-kootchy, two
Janes for the price of one! Could you please stop
while I grovel. Not one of your typical men-in-waiting
this kneeling before betters takes a bit of concentration
of which I'm in short supply. A bevy of ambulances
with pints of blood (donated) could top me up. Which
reminds me: do you identify as fem? Top? Or bottom?
I'm easy; given clearance from the control tower, I'll go
with either if I can place one more conjugal mismatch
in your we-care operation. Sakes alive, ain't that
slave too short on his chain when the grave-talk
leaves off I'll get with your country & western
*Hey that wall never did look right whatever
it's keepin' in I don't want to know*: that
What is written it stinks of a book.

Philip Hammial

Morning Meeting

He tells me that
this is his sacred place.

He tells me that
he comes to Gettysburg twice a year.

He tells me that
he's been almost forty times.

He tells me that
he's travelled all over,
but this is still his sacred place.

He tells me that
his wife never came to this, his sacred place.

He tells me that
she had no time for this macho war nonsense.

He tells me that
he was here in Gettysburg when his wife died
back home in Montgomery, Missouri.

He tells me that
he'd kissed her goodbye
without any thought that it might be the last time.

He tells me that
he still comes to Gettysburg twice a year
and cries for his dead wife
back home in Montgomery.

James Roy

From Mountain Journal

i.

Grey cover   rain approaching

    I sit and look, imagine the horizon
the moon, the wet green spruce
  no shadow

      Now
a crimson rosella   a drop of blood
            bleeds down
    the narrow arm
      of a scribbly gum

             then another
   three red drops fly
     down into the hollow

I'd like to make a fire here tonight

       In the centre of the hot coil
   it just keeps going.

ii.

   A slender dead trunk
     reaches into the sky, a claw

    hard dry wood
       scratching the brittle blue
    like lightning

       or just fecundity reversed

at the moment
I start to write
all the kookaburras laugh.

iii.

Look at that old oak
    at the front of the school,
cold morning sunlight
    seeing through every grey ring
right to the amber centre

we look at early buds
    already waiting for spring,
close to the eye
    see hardened, withered skin

it hasn't rained for weeks
    you say, an aching dry
& undiluted cold
    sunk down off the mesosphere
each night
    the heat, the cold
killing all the buds.
    Maybe

    it's a very old oak
you say, and look
    (running off)
look at all the evergreens,
    they are always green
that's why they're called
    evergreens.

iv.

The atmosphere resembles
　　　water
　　　neurons like gill lamellae
　　absorb the real
　　　exhale words

　　　condensing as *apple tree, weeping cherry*
　　　　privet, hackberry
　　　tree-ferns, spruce
　　　　　the row of *Italian alders*
　　a stand of *eucalypts*
　　　& dark green
　slabs of *Monterey pines*
　　　near the top of the crest

　　from here
　　I can only see one small house
　in the distance through the trees
　　　its silver iron roof
　　　　white walls
　　　white window frames

　　　　　like a cube of ice
　　　caught in a dark grey net of twigs
　　　　& branches

　　the house is always empty

　　　　　at dusk the donkeys over there
　　　hee-haw

Peter Minter

Mud Season

I will come to my love in mud season, when rain softens the snow
on his side of the globe he wants to grow
a row of fruit trees to block the sound of trucks
heaving down the side road, going too fast.

He has put up a sign: Slow down. Slow down.
Try 20K.

I did slow down when we lay in his attic room, the wood house built
over a century ago when there was still time
for saplings to grow into his imagined future
I cannot see.

I slowed to a stop,
slowed down to now
right now, his body inside me
the sweet smell of him,
like fruit trees in spring.

I will come to my love in mud season,
my boots sucking the earth
when there is no risk of property damage,
no property,
just this.

Carol Major

The New World, 1607

seven ships dropped anchor
dark hulks of unnatural imagining
bearing hope and trepidation

flintlock men alighted
stood uncertain on this empty shore
land-sick and wide-eyed

from across the swamp
where gulping turtles trailed indifference
came murmured scraps of watching

distant night drums
drew glances of envy to the forest
its belly glowing with fire

with that first winter
crept a bone-deep stony hunger
plotting and waiting

a dozen crosses
made of sticks and precious twine
pricked the snow

they huddled close
those few pathetic monuments
to the weak

when spring finally came
deeper graves were dug in the thawing soil
but the stony hunger remained

an easy footbridge now spans
the swamp where turtles sun themselves
with cool indifference

James Roy

Nine Views of Mt Hay

1

New Growth

The fire has been a bearer of largesse
   And, far from human edifice
Or dwelling, was benign, was gently fierce,
   Was merciless yet generous.

For, travelling like a journeyman who works,
   Is paid in ash, moves on, but wreaks
Renewal in the ghost-gum's tangling sticks,
   The fire elicits strangeness, makes

New poplars of each eucalyptus, a glade
   Of quartz to shine in mounds, beside
The blackwood and the blackened branching wood
   Which thrusts out cone and pyramid

Of cellulosic frost in the air,
   Fine-fringed and fimbriate and fair,
Direct and startling as a cactus flower,
   Epiphany in semaphore.

And banksia stems like silver washed in blood
   Burst from its arms a lurid red
While in the hanging swamps the bailiff fire
   Has taken all the furniture

But left the tufted carpet, green and bare,
   Pure celadon. Now, everywhere,
New growth is springing, quickening, from the head,
   Like Lazarus rising from his bed.

2
A Stadium of Stones

Through a tangled, sparring
Forest of fallen spars
Flittering with sparrows,
From Eucalypt agglomerata
Shadow we break out
Circled with bright aggregate
On to a bare plateau
The size of Liechtenstein,
Covered with lichen
And dust of light,
A rock table furnished
With loaves and fishes
Of stone, shale fichus
Pleated with fissures,
A mile-wide
Open kiln of shards
Never in shade
But for clouds:
As if each stares
Only at sky and stars,
Nothing startles or stirs
This plethora of thrones
Where stone rests on stone
And number itself lies strewn
Where it was thrown,
Every stone unturned.

3
Pacific Basin

The tidal wave for twenty million years
Advanced at 7mm per year
Reaching at last Lithgow to the west,

Maitland and Razorback and beyond,
So that, during this aquatic carnival
Which went on for 20,000 millennia,

Fish swam from Colo Vale to Hilltop
Or Newcastle to Picton via Jenolan
Often nudging and dislodging sediment,

And mud poured down from flooded inland rivers
Settling in that windsurfing saucer pool.
All that time, basking in the interested sun

And watching displays of synchronised swimming, or diving
Under fountains or floating out to moored pontoons,
Were traces of future possibility

Which even now persist in these dry stones
Reclining still under the cooling sun,
Indolent along the edges of the drained pool.

4
Extra time

The overhang looks out
On a plateau halfway down to the blue-gum forest
And the snaking river.
It seems to float in space like a cantilevered platform,

And on it is being played
A running game for rocks now into cosmic extra time.
To qualify, a rock must
Have maintained its position for a period of not less
Than a million years
And be marked by one or more expendable silver saplings.
These stand in groups
And contrast with the players by their responsiveness to the weather.
The ledge or playing field
Is half a mile long and almost as wide, and glistens
Against the dark gorge below
Hidden in the smoking shadow of the cliff opposite.
The object of the game
Is to induce vertigo in the opposing monolith so that,
Despite its mass,
It may at last be forced to overtopple into the chasm,
Or by some other stratagem
To occupy the precise space guarded by the other.
This constitutes a score.
But for many millennia play has been set firmly
In defensive patterns
So that the contest is still locked at nil-all;
As yet no mechanism
Has been devised which will resolve this deadlock.
Highlights of the game
Have been recorded and may be read nearby in lichen.
As play see-saws
Between one hump-backed whale-white contender and another,
A gallery of stones,
Many standing on the backs of others to observe the arena,
Appears animated, almost
To the point of crowding to the brink of expectation
Of an imminent result.

5
Winter Collections

Inconsolable Number finding itself
In every theatre or domain outnumbered

Even to the point of abandoning all idea
Of assigning tokens to every branch.

A rock ledge like a coastline.
A steeply sloping tennis court.

An incline from which water
Does not move. A rock ledge.
A sedge like a deodar
The colour of jeweller's rouge
Standing on this coastline.

A bleached branch
Like a stick-insect,
A stone like a moth,
A bird like a stone.
A spray of gorse
Like branches of rain
Across a valley.
A circular indentation
Delicate and as shallow
As a ring-worm mark
Or inoculation scar,
Housing a single pebble.

An armchair of rock.
A shale day-bed facing the sun.

A seedling growing on rock
Chrome-orange fringed.
A pierced garden roller
Made of ironstone.

The paler shadows of black crows scud
Over the sedge field

Granite hayricks,
Feathers under tarpaulins.

The raised back
Of a basking hippopotamus

Or elephant
Or kangaroo
Or potaroo.

Theatre of events
Where by events
We mean the residue
Of past events
Now cloaked in stone.

The shadows of crows
Scud more palely
Over the sedge field.

6
Tableaux

In the mile-wide auditorium
Above the snaking river

A single termite mound
Is the only obelisk.

Bearing no inscription
It shares with this place

The ancient absence of
Constructed languages

Other than those traces
Brought in by visitors.

Those echoes rapidly fade
Leaving always the sound

Of the tasselled wind from the gorge,
Pre-verbal and persuasive,

Promising a theatre of events
Decisive, unsyllogistic,

Pure, quite uncontingent.
This will culminate

In a widening gap between
Cause and effect, and at last

A finale for the whole company—
Tree, rock and sky—

In which existence and essence
Exactly coincide.

7
A Scientific Prospect

It may well be that, in our lifetime, we
The heirs of Galileo, may yet see
The founding ferment of this stone,
This

      valley, these clefts and ledges and unfurled flans,
      eaves and tiles and capping ridges of sandstone,
      the formation of ironstone all-sorts from which fondant
      has long been weathered, the origin of theatres
      and curious corridors and mazes formed by upheaval,
      extruded platforms above which an eagle floats slowly
      on thermal currents, these long-waisted rocks at
      the moment of encirclement by girdles of quartz;
We merely need to find one floating moon
Or spiral arm which holds aloft a screen
So far away that light rays from our sun
Which passed here as that heaving flood began
Reflect upon it and return.
That place

      must be the precise number of light-years distant
      so that reflections reaching us here may carry
      their images of those days of formative cataclysm.
      Scanners resolve and relay to monitors those images,
      and we observe the earth like a fruit
      casting out its pith and peel of stones.
      Should this, the ultimate atavism, come to pass,

For this, it might be most appropriate
If television monitors were set
Here in this vast effusion of stone shards,
And deck chairs spread amongst these ironstone curds
Which have stood still as, all the while, these rays
Have travelled and returned from distant stars,
Bearing these ancient photographs.

8
Fugitive Remains

Imposing the pastoral
On the primeval,
   The absence of trees

Allows a path
To stretch ahead
   Towards the ravine edge

Drawing us into
Memories of fields,
   Difficult versions of Arcadia.

Figurative presences, fallen
Creatures of stone
   Line the winding path

As if once
An entire community
   Ascending from the underworld,

Almost breaking free
Has been vitrified
   By many backward glances.

9
A Dialogue as Coda

Over the dromedary skyline came the first
Breezes of raincloud, as wide cirrus skies
Contracted and billowed into cumulus marble;

Here, where light richocheted from leonine rocks
Back to those clouds, a discussion was taking place
Which would lead to an unexpected comparison.

"Nothing here on this thin plateau between valleys,"
Said one speaker choosing a negative universal
To affirm positively the uniqueness of this place,

"Can be described," (and here he strayed to the brink
And stood looking down at the indigo shadows
Of the canyon and its silver winding river)

"Since there must always be those ultimates
—This place is one—in terms of whose beauty others
May be suggested but which themselves..." and he continued

To expatiate at great length and to little effect.
"But this is not actually true," said the second, joining him
On an outer ledge of pale powdered stone

Littered with clinker. "Some likenesses are possible.
Consider these fragments of dark scoriform ironstone, lying
Like bread crusts left after a multitudinous feast.

Are they not precisely like the sepals of Iceland poppies
Which having fallen from their opening buds are caught
Across stamens and in the creases of petals?"

"You are right, said the first, smiling. "Even here, everything
Has its likeness in something dissimilar somewhere else;
In fact, that feeling of afterthought which these shards induce,

As if they were ardently inclined to persist in our thought
Beyond the allotted period of their being seen,
Is quite like noting the poppies' perfume of wild honey."

John Watson

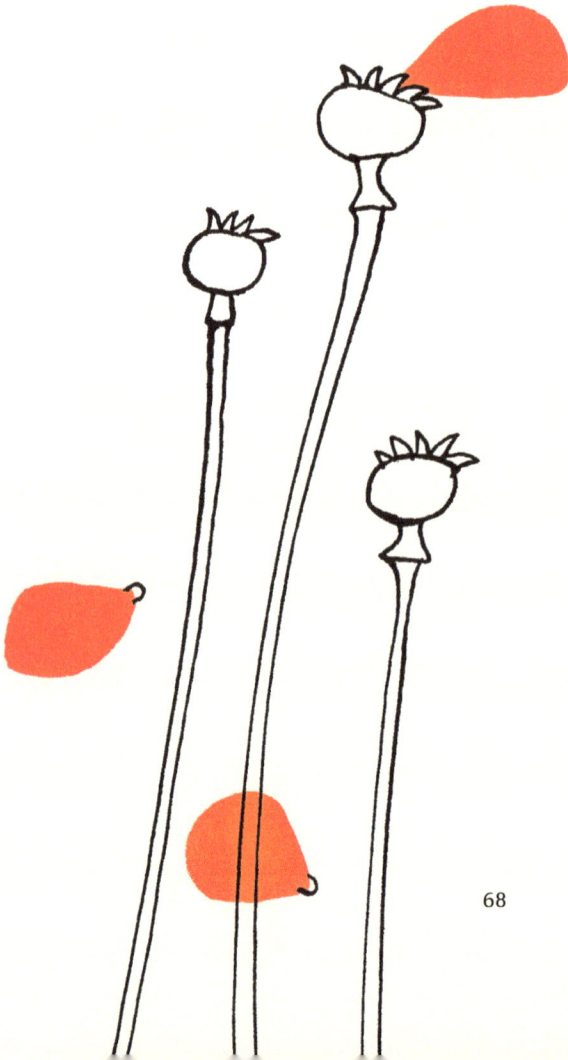

# of glass and wood and water

I am trying to tell you about Venice,
how I felt
waking in a crisp white room
to rain falling softly
in the courtyard
outside my window.

I want to tell you about the light in that room,
about the houseplants and the glass
and the books
in languages I couldn't read
and the bath that didn't work,
how happy I was.

I want to tell you about the colour of Venetian water
and the way the sky and sea
makes everything soft and old,
how the wood groans—
the way nothing is spoken
and everything is sung.

In Venice I walked on wet stone
through a floating cloud.
You weren't there,
so the mist kissed the back of my neck
where you would have.

Emma Brazil

Pinecones

The great sequoia rushes slowly up.
You bring it from a burning north,
counterpoint to *fastigata* gums
that cap the basalt peaks,
geologic time in their limbs.
Housed or free, a single germ
carries a mighty trunk.

My daughter hides among sprouts
at the redwood base. *Sempervirens*,
echoes of a parent century,
tall and green like memories grown
for children yet to arrive.
We drift under conifers, our feet
soft as nightjars on needles.

One pinecone is a wooden rose.
She carefully knocks a clutch of seeds
from its scales, aligns
a dozen on her palm, each a pyramid
waiting to be born. *If I plant these
we can come back and see
when I'm older than this garden.*

Kate Fagan

The poet imbibes

something happened a long way from here and long long ago

no witnesses
the echo died out in the void

some owl hooted some pale stars blinked
there was a muffled sound that quickly soughed into the earth

it had to happen:
nothing would be the same if it hadn't

don't look at me like that
these words may never have found each other space and time

might have even drifted apart

what do you know anyway?

the two need an event
like a fraught couple needs a child

something happened, is all I'm saying some tree fell in the dark forest
and no-one heard no-one saw no-one cared and we are all its echo

Justin Lowe

Radiata /Elphinstone Plateau

The Radiata Pines are dying out there.
They do not belong, unmanaged and unkept,
in an unfamiliar landscape, they fall.
It is bush, it is a forest,
regaining pristineness.
Sacred Land.

The mother tree drops her seed,
creating a new growth of Eucalypt.
The twin trees that previously marked
the path down into the Megalong Valley
no longer stand alone.
The Mountain Ash grows tall.

Hermits lived out there.
Secret passages into other worlds.
The magnitudes of forests,
enchantments of that primal energy.
The intent to become
had been disrupted, bulldozed.

The habitat regains its own volition.
Geebungs, Casuarinas and Hakeas.
Hopbush and Conebush and Bottlebrush,
Wattles and Banksias.
All vibrant and strong.
Declaring a homecoming.

The land announces itself with birds
and wind and bustles in the undergrowth.
We must protect it! Hold its intent as sacred.
Forest oh forest!
May you remain unspoiled.

Kasia Olszewski

The Roadside Bramble

Walking late by a roadside bramble
Hoops of brittle thorn, a caul of dead grass, quiet rust
Frost-burnt une feuille serrate
Motes fall and swirl as brassy notes and cobwebs
Tangle straw stems in mossy dirt, the gravel wash
A stripped page of newspaper rotting, crushed
Polyethylene terephthalate
Half-full of piss or rain water, the sign of a dog
Chalk eroded in the furrow of a wheel
Gone a little wide on the corner, or a near miss
Now overgrown in parochial paspalum, afternoon light
Cold and real, bees somewhere in the shadows
A thought of honey in the thicket
The grey common behind a wire fence half down in the damp
Bruise hung on the smoke
Of a sundog burnt in hazy sky, translucent
Sleep stuck in the cavernous dawn of a bramble there by the roadside
Where I hurry into the emaciated past
Where dry straw recedes speechless into the middle distance
A skein of mist settling over a paddock
Air still, damp, muddy in my nose as the scent of blood
Steel cold hockey bone blue, knee high
Twigs and the hair on my skin lift in the golden aperture
Of the sky's milk crystal
Fanned behind a brittle stand of eight grey poplars
Pines melting in the middle distance
Dark green glass shards sliding into the earth
A path trodden flakes of rock
Through clumps and bristles of grass and wet-stemmed seed-heads
Drooping over bright plastic bits and rusting caps
Squashed with dirt into a bleak loam
A field scattered with the bones of my predecessors

Wandering aimlessly over turquoise hills, smoky dead trees
I find I'm outside the future, overgrown
Great walls of roots & earth crumbling sodden in the muddy weather
Wooden claws of hackberry gum
Knotted foetal in the grey wind, contrail chords in the sky
Lines unfurling between hard matter and blue
Blown above a jetliner's silver precipice
Disappearing into the end of a broken branch
Time and space are orange as mud in gravel
Trees a-glint with a wild fire
Sparks flying across the horizon the singular grey abyss
Every bramble has been the same, I think
As they all rush from my past like black swans, snow geese
Drawn into the circle of gravel
A formation of birds dropping suddenly into mind
As I walk around, feathers widening
Angular as they land into the poverty of the world
The horizon always looming, then retreating from the present
And all it holds, the skeletal frame of a sparrow chick
Its absent eye resting on a quartz pebble
Left as a sign to the logic of inhuman death, clear, immensely old
A grain of cold stone, the indifferent raw tangle
In a bracken fern halo, the silent forehead of a sickle moon
Tacked strangely to a wooden light-pole
The sound of water tinkling and gurgling, treble & bass
A silver banner fluttering and wending
Through the poplars and brace of pines
Darkness somehow equal to its bright and random melody
Caught in the cold pomegranate at the road's end
Crimson flesh held in a world of white foam
Mist correlates, transpires, solid shapes beneath the moon
& stars, hips and haws, love and hate

No matter how opaque and powerless I become
I still cry into the night as it springs burning into felony
Emptiness glowing through dry yellow stalks
No match for the whorl at the crown of your head
Telescoped to a galaxy, a whale from the old world bare
As a chunky key-ring nob lost in the mossy grit
Where I walk & look, no doubt within
Perhaps hell-bent as gravel paths spread from me chaotically
All the same, having wandered here before
And knowing how each will always yield its own
I fall away into the roadside ditch
Sticks and mud stuck in my hair, the back of my throat
Catching the gold sunset
Behind, of course, bitumen spread Bauhaus thin and black
A wall of glass windows over the road
A mercury pool shimmering in the wind
The whole reflected world shuddering.

Peter Minter

St Kitts

and all the promises
the bee hums to the blushing flower

all the sly plans of butter-fed stars
the jagged architecture of wind in the leeward trees

the plantation talk of margins
and of markets that grow more distant

with each new war each passing year

and Venus low in the east
and jungle birds sallow in the cold eye of the hurricane

and the native girls
coaxing a tune out of old rum bottles

swivelling their hips wide as morning laughing like rain down a hillside

and all the white knuckled prayers on the slow ride into town

grasping for a coin of sunlight on the valley floor

Justin Lowe

The Seamstress

she listens to the faint trickling in the ceiling pipes as the share
rider in 4D scrubs away his nightshift

the pipes chatter as though the shards
of a shattered glass man were being washed down the plughole

outside the sky brightens
the storm clouds blush as they retreat out to sea

the sea is a rumour the gulls bring to her railing

and on a warm day she thinks she can smell it

like the armpits of her mother as she sewed
gazed sadly at the piles of boxes through a cloud of nicotine

sometimes she could play for an hour in those boxes
but then she would be ordered to fill them with the night noise

the gentle whirr that lulled her to sleep
and they would eat and wait for the knock at the door

the silent exchange of one box for another
in every package that she opens sleeps the sad smile of her mother

Justin Lowe

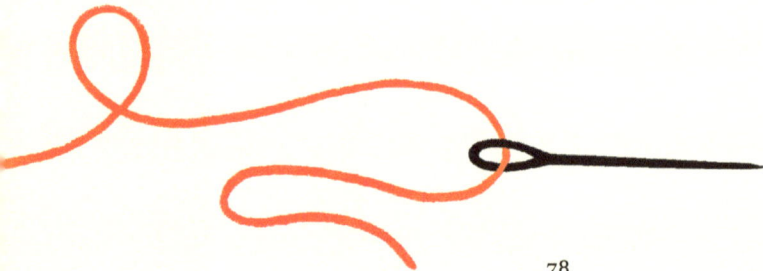

Shipley Winter Trees

After Peter Rushforth: A Legacy – Blue Mountains Cultural Centre
2019 ceramic bowl 'Shipley Winter Trees'

White rivers curving tributaries leaking into fine veins.
Finger trunk polished, striped winter sun not finding south.

Reflection past the Perspex box, warped self looms.
Spherical light pushes elsewhere.
Crazed egg-shell blue breaks dawn-dusk time.

Smoke bush brain lights with memory trees;
a dancer, chest up, arms back
one leg, toe pointing skyward.
Bach cello echoes against the corridors of wood.

Meredith Pitt

From **Song in the Grass**

The day is quiet now
I sit with a lamp, circled by pages
It's physical work to remain within this orbit and voyage
        as though my skull were oceans

Cliffs keeling
Neophytes dropping to ancestral floods

The gabions stave off the weather
It took years to pack them
Gale music is scored in rattling wire, a common song
        of oars lashed by rain
The erratic compass

I've stood on Treachery Head and heard what isn't there
Bodies emptied by sea and rowed to rest, floorboards
        primed with salt and tears

Beyond the dark is a kind of seeing
Time's experiment

The north easterlies whine
I'm drawn to the hill behind our shed where a giant gum
        wheels and lifts
For days I pinch out privet and blackberry
Fierce holly and hawksbeard
A lyrical index

Language falling from leaves: koel and spinebill, fan-tailed
        cuckoo, golden whistler
Water in a broken gutter
The instruments have turned into birds

The roof is an accordion with a 23-screw fingerboard
        and tin bellows

Kate Fagan

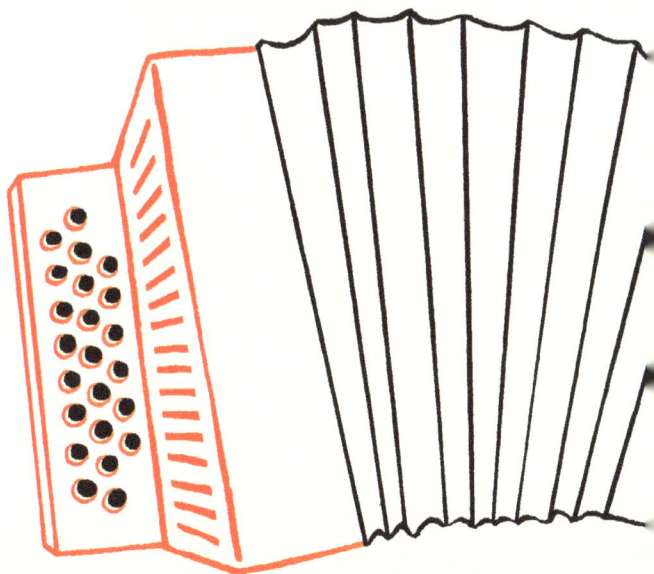

Sublime Point

Standing at
Sublime Point, looking out,
is like death
or sudden viciousness, access
to a beauty
that you'd never thought you'd have,
an idea that changes everything.

Rock-shelves
crumble into the distant scrub,
birds
dive into a sea of hieroglyphs
dense as an empty page.

Standing at
Sublime Point
you find yourself longing for the arrival of the lost,
a cure for the illness you think you will die from,
someone to hold you
who will excite you forever

clinging
too fast to the guard-rail
as if it were a strong
line around you, a second skin
holding the vastness in.

David Brooks

Take

Take a break, a seat, a consequence seat, in it a hot-
under-the-collar hero at market value with a promise
of a life of glee, an endowed hero armed with
a glad rag what a way to go.

Take a chance, a lacklustre, a lockdown, a limousine
door opened by a chauffeur, a descending stiletto,
a well-turned ankle, a gaggle of leering men
what a shame to crow.

Take a dare, an exultation, an entourage of bit players
incurring the wrath of a mad queen, her rage the stuff
of hoopla, of hoosegow, of hop & skip's haute couture
What a face to throw.

Take a bow, a plumage, a scold, a proxy indulged
with a squandering, a scrub to within an inch, a heartfelt
rub it won't take long, seven years at the most & by then
what a hit by a foe.

Take a pick, a spin, a penny farthing, a ride
to a rendezvous with a Miss Joyce Lee, her plunder
your blunder, no you won't get another chance
what a low blow.

Take a tune, a rune, a broom to sweep what you've done
under a rug, a thug for a pal, an exemption for
the castrato in your bed on whose account you'll pay
as you go what a lovely glow.

Philip Hammial

Ten Towns Down

Those sounds again, each night,
over and over as the dark unfolds, great
punchings and shudderings of air, as if
squadrons of dragons were taking flight,

such screechings and clangings as might attest
the closing of the seven gates of Hell,
thunderings, like the stampede
of a thousand wildebeest

or moanings, like the lonely
calvings of a glacier – but no, it's only
the coal train from Lithgow
as it crests the range, begins the slow

descent towards Sydney, hauls
its thousand tonnes of cold black fire
through Katoomba, Leura, Wentworth Falls
and our dreams with them, all the ten towns down.

David Brooks

Über Frankfurt

I imagine
that I am floating
six floors up—
framed on this bed
—and not as I am
in a small white apartment,
downtown Frankfurt,
in a weary gravy
of half sleep.
Just hovering here—
on thick grey air
punctured by sound
from police sirens,
church bells,
cars, lorries
and voices
bellow
speaking
in foreign languages
—at home it's October and
white cockatoos will be resting
amongst the loose pink blossoms
in our cherry tree.

Faye Wilson

Welcome Table, Blackheath

Choose a house, a tree or two, maybe a dog or a dragon
pack them in a hold-all, drag them through the streets
wear down the corners, leave stray branches or a fence paling
in meetings and on buses, trail the spume of escape.

Climb towards the copper beeches, the lit logs and white, frosty
roads. Rickety, sticky, ring-barked table in the local pub.

There's a place
for us. We've left our suits, buried our parents—
abandoned the anthills filled with people or paint or a thousand masks.
Our otherness becomes belonging, we are choreographed in-situ,
never still, knocking knees, hands across other's backs;
we pass show-and-tell around the table.

Chairs as breath, in and out, added to form a bump, then taken to a dent—
coats abandoned over the back of seats left.

Rubies needing to be shared, the dance of new friends,
I relish the recognition in the faces as I arrive.

I am the incomer, still to learn how many thermals, where to find petrol
still shedding the tell-tale signs of city life. I scribble where the best
charity shop is to dump the detritus of a past left, discover the art
of blackouts, ice on the windscreen, on the road and on the railing gripped
in a moment, slipping.

Meredith Pitt

Wild Duck Sutra

Eight wild wood ducks
greet me at the gate,
follow me down to the feed-room, wait
while I get them a handful of seed
before taking hay to the sheep
who descend upon it as if it were the last
lucerne in the country

I stand and watch
then leave them to it, walk off
to fill the water trough
the sky clearing
in more ways than meet the eye
the world outside these fences
so precariously at bay

it hardly bears thinking: all
things are full of meaning, so
they say, you just
have to wait for it;
what they don't say
is how much you have to clear away
before the simplest things become evident

as this, for example,
dripping from the lip of the tank,
creeping like the sunlight
over the grass, slipping
from the beaks of wood-ducks: how
we might share refuge, rescue
each other

David Brooks

Witching Hour

Icing sits on the cake of an old tyre
by the side of the frozen road.
Birds drift like shoals of fish
over green reefs of mountain ash
turning as one in the light disappearing,
turning again, swirling
in the disturbed current of the air.
Before long the moon will loose
its knucklebone into the sky.

The distant trees hold rhinestones
of cockatoos, each a flake
of desiccated coconut croaking
'Cold, cold,' with the sound of nails
being drawn from dried timber.
In the first valley night
has already stumbled to its knees.
On the far side light in a single
window, a single quill of smoke.

Mark O'Flynn

Woman on Katoomba Street

Passing,
I see something golden in her mouth,
neither tooth nor part of a tooth,

neither filling nor crown,
neither Greek nor Chinese coin,
not a pennyweight

from Witwatersrand,
neither breast of nesting finch
nor signet ring,

not Aristotle's mean,
not slipper, not ticket, not fleece,
but rather

something from within,
aglow, still rising,
something in which,

henceforth,
I shall believe.

Craig Billingham

Contributors' Biographies

Craig Billingham has published two collections of poems, *Storytelling* (2007) and *Public Transport* (2017), as well as numerous short stories, essays and reviews.

Emma Brazil is a poet and teacher whose writing has been published and performed in a variety of settings, including the Sydney Writers' Festival. She holds a Master of Arts (Creative Writing) from the University of Technology, Sydney.

David Brooks is an essayist and fiction writer as well as poet. His latest books are *Open House* (poetry), *Napoleon's Roads* (short stories), *The Grass Library* (meditations on living with animals in the Blue Mountains) and *Animal Dreams* (selected essays). He lives with rescued sheep on a small property on the outskirts of Katoomba.

Kate Fagan is a widely published writer, musician and academic whose third volume, *First Light*, was shortlisted for the NSW Premier's Literary Awards and the Age Book of the Year Award. She is a former editor of *How2*, the US journal of contemporary poetry and scholarship, and an internationally acclaimed songwriter whose album *Diamond Wheel* won the National Film and Sound Archive Award for Folk Recording. She is Director of the Writing and Society Research Centre at Western Sydney University.

Philip Hammial has published 28 collections of poetry. Born in Detroit, he has represented Australia at twelve international poetry festivals. He is also an outsider artist and sculptor, and a director of Island Press.

Vanessa Kirkpatrick is a poet, teacher, and writing consultant. Her first collection, *To Catch the Light* (2013), won the inaugural John Knight Poetry Manuscript Prize and was commended for the Anne Elder Award for best debut collection. Her second collection, *The Conversation of Trees*, was published in 2017.

Sheridan Linnell participated in Varuna's local mentorship program with Deb Westbury, then in the Wollongong poetry workshops with Five Island Press. Sheridan's book *Cutting Room* was published in *New Poets 6*. While working at Western Sydney University, Sheridan has found every possible excuse to weave poetry, memoir and creative non-fiction into academic writing. An alumni residency at Varuna in 2019 reminded her that no excuses are needed for doing what she loves.

Justin Lowe lives in a house called "Doug" where he edits the international poetry blog, *Bluepepper*. His work has appeared recently in *Meanjin, Stylus Journal, Cortland Review* (USA) and *Blue Nib* (UK). He has also had poems set to music by bands including The Whitlams and The Impossibles.

Carol Major was born in Scotland, later completed her education in Canada and now lives in Australia. Her short stories and poems have been published in Canadian and Australian journals, and she has authored numerous articles on health care, social policy and urban design. Her memoir *The Asparagus Wars* was recently published by ES-PRESS, an imprint of Spineless Wonders publishing. Carol is an alumna and valued mentor at Varuna, Australia's National Writers House.

Peter Minter is a poet, poetry editor and writer on poetry and poetics. He teaches at the University of Sydney.

Mark O'Flynn has published several collections of poetry, most recently *The Soup's Song* (Picaro, 2015), and *Shared Breath* (Hope St. Press 2017). His novels include *Grassdogs* (2006), *The Forgotten World* (2013), and *The Last Days of Ava Langdon* (UQP, 2016) which was shortlisted for the Miles Franklin Award and the Prime Minister's Award for fiction, as well as winning the Voss Literary Award in 2017. His latest collection of short stories is *Dental Tourism*, published by Puncher and Wattmann.

Kasia Olszewski is a theatre practitioner who lives in Katoomba. She is passionate about environmental sustainability. She self published a poetry anthology in 2018.

Meredith Pitt is a poet who has been published in various print and online journals, most recently *Not Very Quiet* and *Cicerone*.

Michelle Rickerby was once a writer/producer of short form content for children's television, and wrote film reviews in London. She held senior roles at ABC Commercial and WestWords, hanging art exhibitions and producing literary events across greater western Sydney. These days she practises writing and editing from home.

James Roy is a writer and musician. His published work includes fiction, historical fiction, poetry, children's television, and libretto, and his books for young people have won four Premier's Awards, and a German Youth Literature Prize nomination.

Michel Streich is an illustrator, working mainly for publishers of magazines and books. Born and educated in Germany, he started his illustration career in London, and moved to Australia in 2000. He is the author of several children's books and has a passion for book design.

John Watson was formerly a teacher of mathematics (mentioning Fibonacci whenever possible), it being a less intrusive subject to teach if one wishes to versify. His poetry prizes include the Newcastle, Blake Poetry Prize, Josephine Ulrick and the Bruce Dawe poetry prizes. Amongst 100 published books, several are with Puncher and Wattmann or Ginninderra, while many are chap-books (with Picaro/ Ginninderra), small enough for the reader to hold in one hand without relinquishing the smart phone in the other. He represented Australia at the International Poetry Festival at Trois Rivieres in 2012.

Faye Wilson is a multi-disciplined artist with an abiding interest in the marriage of image and text. After participating in a Varuna mentorship program with Deb Westbury, a book of her poems, paintings and photographs *Snow on a Black Dog's Back* was published in 2001. Since then Faye has brought poets and artists together for the Black + Blue 1 and 2 exhibitions at Blue Mountains Cultural Centre, held several solo shows, and produced the independent arts magazine, *Blume Illustrated*.

* * *

The Blue Mountains **City of the Arts Trust**, whose support made this book project possible, was created to build on the City's reputation of being the inaugural City of the Arts in NSW. The Trust's primary objectives are to support the local arts industry and strengthen the cultural fabric of the Blue Mountains, encourage arts quality and innovation, and engage local communities and visitors in arts and cultural activities, as both participants and audiences.
The Trust Advisory Committee makes recommendations to the Blue Mountains City Council each year to support selected arts projects in the visual, performing and literary arts for the benefit of Blue Mountains residents.

Publishing Credits

Sublime Point by David Brooks was published in his *Urban Elegies* (Island Press, 2007), *Ten Towns Down* and *Driving Home* in his *Open House* (University of Queensland Press, 2016), and *Wild Duck Sutra* in the journal *Meanjin*.

Kate Fagan's poem *Heart Sayings* was first published in *Wasafiri: International Contemporary Writing*, Volume 31, Issue 2, June 2016. *Hope Stone: Cento for Felix Minter* was first published in *Arc*, Volume 75, Autumn 2014. *Pinecones* was commissioned for Red Room Poetry's *New Shoots: Blue Mountains Botanic Garden Project* and was first published online by Red Room Poetry in November 2017. *Song in the Grass* was commissioned by Irish writer Dermot Healy for the volume *Writing the Sky: Observations and Essays on Dermot Healy*, edited by C.A. Murphy and K. Hopper, and first published by Dalkey Archive Press in 2016.

Phil Hammial's poems are from his latest book, *Squandering Veronicas* (Island Press, 2020)

Vanessa Kirkpatrick's *The Blue Gum Forest* was first published in her book *The Conversation of Trees* (Hope Street Press), and *Last Summer* was broadcast on ABC Radio National Breakfast, 27 November 2020;

Peter Minter's poem *The Clearing* was first published in *Rabbit* number 6, Melbourne, pp. 55-56. *The Roadside Bramble* was first published in *Southerly*, Volume 72, Issue 1, 72 (1), Sydney, pp. 84-86 (English Association, Sydney Branch, 2012).

Mark O'Flynn's poem *Grasshopper, 1889* was first published in *Verity La*, 2020. *Incident at Mt Boyce* previously appeared in *What Can Be Proven* (IP Press, 2007). *Bushwalking for Beginners* appeared in *Untested Cures for Modern Day Ailments* (Picaro Press, 2011). *Witching Hour* was published in *The Soup's Song* (Picaro Press, 2015).

Kasia Olszewski's poem *Radiata / Elphinstone Plateau* refers to a plateau on the outskirts of Katoomba that is now protected. After 30 years of community activism the plateau was, in 2019, acquired by the NSW National Parks and Wildlife Service and made into a Regional Park. It was renamed *Ngula Bulgarabang* meaning 'Very large wood forest.'

John Watson's *9 Views of Mt Hay*, was initially published in *A First Reader* (Brandl & Schlesinger).

www.ingramcontent.com/pod-product-compliance
Lightning Source LLC
Chambersburg PA
CBHW040804150426

42811CB00082B/2391/J